HOW TO SPEAK

Dog

HOW TO SPEAK DOG

An exclusive edition for

for all your gift books and gift stationery

This edition first published in Great Britain in 2018 by
Allsorted Ltd, Watford, Herts, UK WD19 4BG

© Susanna Geoghegan Gift Publishing

Author: Helen Redding with contribution from MIchael Powell.

Cover design: Milestone Creative

Contents design: Double Fish Design Ltd

ISBN: 978-1-911517-56-6

Printed in China

HOW TO SPEAK

Dog

Understand
what your
dog is trying
to tell you

Contents

A MEETING OF MINDS

BODY SENSE

SENSES

I'M LISTENING

GROWING TOGETHER

A person who has never owned a dog has missed a wonderful part of life.

BOB BARKER

Introduction

Whether you've owned a dog for years or are a complete novice, by the end of this book you'll understand the amazing ways in which your dog interacts with the world and with you. You may be called a dog 'owner', but you're actually one half of a partnership. For this partnership to be successful, you need to be able to interpret what your dog is telling you. What does that rapid, high-pitched bark mean? Is their tail wagging like that a good sign? Are they really feeling guilty for stealing the leftovers you were saving for tomorrow? Effective communication between you and your dog has a crucial part to play in your dog's good behaviour and happiness.

Dogs are wonderful creatures. They want to please you by giving you sloppy kisses and, if you're lucky, bringing you their favourite, and mankiest, chew toy. In return, all they ask for is love and attention ... and food. When you understand your dog's behaviour and how they see the world, you can build that all-important bond between you. And if you keep your side of the bargain, it will be a bond for life.

You cannot share your life with a dog ... and not know perfectly well that animals have personalities and minds and feelings.

JANE GOODALL

A MEETING OF

Minds

ALL DOGS ARE

Unique

Just like humans, all dogs are unique. They have different personalities, needs, levels of confidence and intelligence. But they are all the same in one respect: they all need an attentive, responsive and responsible owner to keep them safe, secure, happy and healthy. That's YOU, by the way, as well as everyone else in your home. It's a big responsibility.

This book doesn't go into the usual detail about the nitty-gritty of dog ownership, like choosing the right dog food to buying engaging toys. Instead, it focuses on observation and communication. Its primary aim is to help you to understand how your dog interacts with and interprets the world through its senses. It will help you to be more aware of the many ways in which your dog communicates with you and with other dogs. Not only will you gain a fascinating glimpse into your dog's world, but you'll have a better appreciation for how she expresses her needs and wants. And with that information, she'll expect you to pander to her every whim!

The more you understand how your dog functions and interacts with its environment, the better you will be able to cater for her needs and live harmoniously with your canine friend. You and your dog may share a home, but you experience it in very different ways. You operate on one physical level, living in your head, which is usually several feet above the floor; your dog's domain extends from the doormat (ready to catch the mail) to the kitchen countertop, even though you think she dwells mainly under your feet!

It's great to feel that our pets are important members of our family, but that doesn't mean that we should treat them like humans. They aren't a lesser priority – they should of course be treated with the same respect, thoughtfulness and sensitivity as you would hope to be shown yourself – but trying to understand them human-centrically is very limited. You must climb a little way into their world.

Breed Characteristics

Whilst all dogs are unique, your dog's breed will to some extent influence its character and behaviour. Entire books have been written on dog breeds – there's been so much selective breeding it makes for fascinating reading – but there isn't the space to discuss them in detail here. You should learn the key characteristics, special requirements and any possible complications associated with your breed before you bring your dog home, since even the simplest factors will dictate how you should care for them.

For example, hair length usually determines how and how often your dog needs to be groomed; a short-haired and smooth-coated dog such as a Whippet only needs grooming once a week, whereas a big, hairy dog like a Briard might have you grooming it in front of the television every night.

If you want to introduce a dog into a family home with children, you should ensure that you choose the right breed, looking at the temperament of different breeds and any special care required. According to David Alderton, author of *Understanding Your Dog,* 'it is vital that you delve carefully into the ancestry of breeds that interest you to gain a clear insight into their behaviour before taking on a canine companion, rather than simply being seduced by a cute appearance. You need to match the needs of your pet to your lifestyle.' In *Being A Dog,* Kate Wild describes how the results of different breeding paths fascinate us: 'Does the way a dog looks influence the way he behaves, or are there other, equally important factors?'.

It is fair to say that certain breeds tend to display distinct characteristics. Breeds of working dogs, thanks to their ancestry, may find it hard to settle into the role of affectionate pet. Sheepdogs, for example, tend to get bored easily if they find themselves holed up in a house without company. Your cushions and furniture will be the first to suffer! Herding dogs, like Border Collies, retain those skills in the stalking and chasing that their ancestors needed for keeping sheep in their place.

Dog enthusiasts will happily tell you which breeds of dog have which characteristics: Corgis are clever, Golden Retrievers are super friendly. But is a dog's breed alone really a reliable way to predict its personality? As Kate Wild says in *Being A Dog,* '"Being a Dog" is not simply a matter of biology – it's an intricate mesh of genetics, learning, appearance and behaviour.' Your dog's behaviour is influenced by its environment, just like your behaviour is.

PUPPYHOOD AND THE BONDING LANGUAGE

of Touch

The strong bond you form with your dog during puppyhood is the basis for your future relationship, so it's important to get things right early on. A puppy is intensely affected by her early experiences and it's vital that you understand and respond positively to her needs to give her a secure foundation.

Typically, your puppy will arrive from a breeder at about eight weeks old. Puppies shouldn't be separated from their mother and litter any earlier than that as those initial social bonds are crucial to a puppy's development. Touch is the first sense that a puppy explores, for example through the comfort that nuzzling can bring and to stimulate milk flow for feeding.

Touch is a great way to communicate with your puppy and to build that all important bond of trust. It can help your puppy to stay calm, make her more social and even increase her ability to learn. The benefits are endless. A properly socialized pup will grow into a well-behaved dog.

Try to stroke her as much as possible and encourage everyone in the family to do the same. The best way to stroke a puppy is by starting at the top of her head and then running your hand down the length of her body.

Pick up your puppy by placing both hands on her chest, behind her front legs. As you bring her towards your chest, move one hand back to support her rear end and leave the other behind her front legs to support her chest. You can then support your puppy by cradling her with both arms. Don't leave any legs dangling or she'll feel unsafe. Hold her firmly but gently and put her down the moment she starts to struggle.

As your puppy grows to trust your touch, remember that there will be times when your attention isn't welcome. Learn to recognize the signs that your dog doesn't want to be touched, for example her body may stiffen, or she may simply move away from your hand. You will also discover that there are certain parts of her body she doesn't like you touching, so respect that and head instead to where you know she loves to be rubbed.

A quiet Homecoming

When you bring your puppy home for the first time, be aware that being taken away from his mother, his siblings and home he was familiar with will make him nervous. Introduce him to a quiet room where he won't be alarmed by loud noises or hoards of people. It's a huge adjustment for both of you, so for the first few days keep the mood calm.

Your puppy will need your undivided attention. Spend time showing him around the house (he'll want to sniff everything at his own pace) and playing with him. If he gets anxious – don't forget that puppies tend to pee if they are – take time to comfort him until he's calm again. A blanket that smells of his mum is a good way to introduce your puppy to his sleeping place. And if he wants to sleep, do let him sleep.

Expect mess and don't get cross with your puppy if (or when!) they have an accident. Ignore the puddles and heap plenty of praise on your puppy when he does go where he's supposed to. Take him into the garden every half an hour or so and after meals and put plenty of newspaper down inside. Get into this routine and you're on your way to potty training your puppy.

Puppies are prone to upset tummies and the new environment and stress of change adds to the risk. You can reduce the risk by feeding your puppy little and often to start with. If you can, feed him the same food he's been used to. Once he's settled in, you can introduce a new food gradually if you want to.

You will no doubt have already been warned that bringing home a puppy is like having a newborn baby (but without the diapers). Be prepared for a few sleepless nights as your puppy gets used to being on his own at night. Initially, he'll be restless and will probably whimper through the night. When you go to check on him, only go in the room when he's quiet. By doing this, your puppy will learn that quiet behaviour, rather than crying, is rewarded with attention. The first few nights will probably be tough but be patient, your puppy will soon start to feel at home and learn to self-soothe.

ESPECIALLY

For You

Did you know that dogs have facial expressions that they use specifically with humans (see page 58)? Yes, those cute puppy dog eyes really are trying to communicate with you (and most probably manipulate you!). Dogs have been working alongside humans for thousands of years so it comes as no surprise how closely connected we are.

It's long been thought that the facial expressions of animals were unconscious movements rather an externalization of emotions or attempts to communicate. However, research has shown that dogs use more facial expressions – such as sticking out their tongue or raising their eyebrows – when they have the attention of humans. As a dog owner, this probably comes as no surprise to you. The look your dog gives you when he's stolen the Sunday roast off the kitchen worktop could really be one of guilt (see page 106) and an attempt to tell you he's sorry.

The unique bond between you and your dog is about more than just communication. It's often commented that people look like their dogs (and vice versa) – it may not be a comparison you're overly happy with but there is some truth to it. Research has shown that people tend to be drawn to dogs that remind them of themselves and pass on their own characteristics to their pet. For example, overweight owners are more likely to have overweight dogs and chilled out owners will have very relaxed dogs. Thankfully, we're more likely to influence our dog's traits than we are to adopt theirs. That saves some embarrassing incidents with lamp posts!

If you want to gain a deeper understanding of how your dog communicates, you need to explore facial expressions, ear and tail positions and other body language signs and visual markers, as well as an entire superculture of smells. All these communication tools will be discussed in greater detail later, so that you can really begin to understand what your dog is thinking and feeling.

As you become more skilled at observing your dog's subtle behaviour, you will deepen the unique bond between you and develop an even greater respect for the incredible creature with whom you have the privilege of sharing your home.

UNIQUE COMMUNICATION BETWEEN
Dog and Owner

As well as understanding the repertoire of barks (see page 94), there are certain elements of communication between dogs and their humans that are unique to that relationship, although they may appear in modified forms elsewhere.

In the tens of thousands of years dogs and humans have existed alongside each other, they've evolved together. It is thought that because domestic dogs have come to rely on humans so much (for food, shelter and protection), they've developed a special skill for interpreting human gestures. This forms the extremely special bond that can be forged between you and your dog. Incredibly, research has found that looking into your dog's eyes produces the same hormonal response that creates our bond with babies.

Your dog spends a huge amount of time with you, so it's not surprising that she's been conditioned to understand you and the complex social interactions that form your daily life together. She is also in tune to your emotions (see page 29). Likewise, as a human you become sensitive and alert to your dog's ways of communicating with you.

Scientific research has shown that dogs have a specific part of their brain that recognizes and differentiates between human faces. The research, conducted at Emory University in the US, was the first to show that an animal other than a primate has this skill. By presenting dogs with different pictures and monitoring their brain response, the scientists found that the paths in dog's brain will 'light up' very differently in response to human faces compared with inanimate objects. If dogs are indeed so in sync with human faces, it helps explain why they are so sensitive to human social cues and have become our best friends.

We can all find things that our dogs do that don't seem to be shared by the general canine population, so there must be personalized touches that arise between two individuals. This can also apply to problems, for example where the owner reinforces antisocial behaviour by making a big deal out of it rather than following the general rule of ignoring unwanted habits and rewarding desirable ones (see page 32). Our unique relationship therefore has its pluses and downsides!

IT ISN'T ALL
About You

Sometimes we can be so busy trying to entertain and get a response from our dogs that we forget to observe and listen. By taking a moment to step back, you will most likely discover that they've been communicating with you all along. It's not all about you – get too caught up in your own pleasure and you'll miss the subtleties of your dog's communication.

For example, nanoseconds after you arrive home, you'll be faced with a wildly excited, tail wagging pooch wanting every ounce of your attention. Depending on your dog, you may also be showered with kisses – the nicer way to describe being covered in dog saliva. This is the wonderful way that dogs say 'hello' and is entirely uninitiated by you. Don't be offended if once that hello is out of the way, she flops back onto her dog bed. Your dog was ecstatic to see you and that took lots of energy; now she needs you to stop fussing.

It can be tempting to show your dog you love her by giving her a hug. Whilst this is a human sign of affection, being hugged can make your dog feel restrained. Read the signs she is giving you before you wade in and invade her space.

There's a huge benefit in staying quiet so that you can be more aware of what your dog is trying to tell you. Be a good listener and a keen observer and you'll quickly learn to understand the ways your dog uses her body and 'voice' to communicate. For example, if your dog brings you her favourite toy it isn't necessarily an invitation to play. By offering you their most prized possession, she's telling you that you're the pack leader. She thinks you'll love a chewed, manky dog toy as much as she does.

When you can understand what your dog is trying to say – and give them the chance to say it – a whole new world opens up. By respecting your dog and taking that step back, you will find that your bond with her strengthens.

Say My Name

Give your dog a name, use it all the time and he'll start to recognize it, yes? Easy! Well, this is part of the process, but there are ways you can do it better if you want him to reliably turn his attention to you when you use his name. Being able to call your dog back is essential and will help him stay out of trouble and danger, and readies him to receive the next command from you.

You need to train your dog so that when you call his name it provokes a happy reaction. To condition this response, always use your dog's name in a positive way and reward him when he responds. Avoid using his name with a negative tone or context. For example, 'Bad Bruno!' or 'Bruno, you're a naughty dog!' are not going to help you train a dog who will happily give you their attention. If he thinks you're angry with him or that there's a punishment on the way, he'll start ignoring you.

When first training your dog to respond to his name, find a quiet room where he can focus entirely on you. Call his name and as soon as you get his attention reward him with some positive words and a small treat. Let his attention move away from you and then try again. Repetition is the name of the game! You'll need to persist with this for a few days but remember that your dog's attention span does have a limit at which point he'll get bored and ignore you.

As your dog gets used to being called, gradually lengthen the time between calling and rewarding him. Take it slowly though; progress too fast and your dog (and you!) may get disheartened. Start calling him in different places and at times when there are added distractions, for example in a room with other family members or whilst he's wearing his lead.

Eventually you'll be able to move it outside – the added levels of distractions may require extra praise and treats. Again, start somewhere quiet and build up from there. Before long, your dog will consistently respond to you calling his name, wherever you are. But beware of overusing his name or it may become just noise to him. Rover? That's his name, don't wear it out!

HOW SMART ARE
Dogs?

Are dogs far cleverer than they're sometimes given credit for? In 2009, research conducted into canine intelligence by animal psychologists in Canada revealed that dogs are as intelligent as an average two-year-old child. The research found that dogs can understand up to 250 words and gestures, count to five and perform simple calculations.

Before you pop *War and Peace* in your dog's basket, the research also found that some breeds of dog are cleverer than others. Dogs bred to follow commands, such as collies and retrievers, are more intelligent that those dogs bred, for example, to hunt for humans. No doubt many dog owners will fight the corner for their own pet's breed, but Border Collies were rated by the research as the most intelligent, whilst Afghan hounds were the least intelligent.

EMPATHY

Have you tried yawning in front of your dog? You may find that she yawns back at you. Yawning is contagious – even with dogs – and is a sign of one of the ways dogs empathize with humans. Dogs are believed to be very sensitive to our emotions and capable of adjusting their behaviour accordingly. Research has also shown that dogs respond to a crying baby in the same way that humans do.

LOVE

Dogs see humans as part of their pack, their family. When your dog seems pleased to see you, he genuinely is. Studies have shown that a dog's brain processes the sound of human voices in the same way that we do. In fact, a little part of their brain lights up when they hear a human voice, especially when it carries an emotive sound like laughter or crying. Dogs are also the only domestic pet to interact with humans as if they are our children. Just like a child, dogs seek out the comfort of a human when they are worried or scared.

Dogs are one of the few animals, apart from apes, who don't interpret eye contact as sign of aggression. When making eye contact, oxytocin – the 'love hormone' – is released. According to Dr Brian Hare, author of *The Genius of Dogs*, this 'is the first time that it has been shown that different species, dog and human, can interact and affect the oxytocin loop.'

UNDERSTANDING GESTURES

Try pointing at something – where does your dog look? Chances are he will look at where you're pointing rather than at your hand. He can also interpret subtler social gestures, such as following your gaze. Amazingly, studies have shown that dogs are better at interpreting human gestures than apes are.

Expressing
Natural behaviours

Whilst dogs love living as part of a pack – your family – they do have to make a compromise to live with us, such as freedom of movement, eating what we choose to give them and obeying our commands. When your dog expresses his natural behaviours, such as digging up the garden, our first reaction is rarely to praise. By knowing what's natural, you'll be better able to understand your dog and manage any problematic behaviour.

CHEWING

You'll have noticed that your dog loves to chew. It's a favourite pastime of puppies whilst they're teething. Rather than lose part of your wall or yet another pair of slippers, make sure your dog has a chew toy in every room to occupy his roving teeth.

BITING

When puppies are playing with their litter, biting is all part of the sibling fun. It's not fun though when it becomes part of their play with you. Don't put up with it! If substituting a chew toy doesn't work, simply stop playing and walk away. He'll soon learn that it's no fun playing by himself.

BARKING

Vocalization is a dog's natural way of communicating. It can be useful (for example, when a stranger knocks at the door) but it can also be extremely annoying. Training is key. Reward your dog when he barks appropriately. When he doesn't (for example, when he barks incessantly at the neighbour's cat), tell him to be quiet and then walk away. He'll gradually learn to only bark for the 'good' reasons.

JUMPING

Jumping is one of the ways that dogs naturally express happiness (see page 54). (Maybe humans should try this more!) However, it's not pleasant for visitors to be jumped up at by a dog, especially one that's been running around a muddy field. Train your dog to know that he can only jump when you give him the signal. Heap on the praise when his four paws are back on solid ground.

Being a responsible dog owner means accepting these and other natural behaviours but directing them so that you can all live happily together under the same roof without repressing your dog's instincts.

USE POSITIVE
Reinforcement

We all love our dogs like members of the family. We enjoy having them around and we want them to be happy, sociable members of our household. That said, they seem to know instinctively how to make our blood pressure rise and make us want to scream and shout. Therefore it's really important to always use positive reinforcement. We know it makes sense, we know it works, but it's so easy to lose the plot and make a bad situation worse and end up with a confused, scolded dog as well as a frustrated owner on the verge of tears.

Positive reinforcement is very simple to understand but can be difficult to fully trust. It means ignoring or deterring bad behaviour and rewarding desirable behaviour. This can be hard to put into practice when you come home to find your new cushions have been ripped to shreds. Losing your temper and shouting or punishing your dog is cruel, it never works (especially since the 'naughty' behaviour might have happened hours ago) and often it can make the problem worse.

It is important to understand what might be causing the unwanted behaviour. The answer is often stress and anxiety or that you have failed to understand your dog's needs. For example, if your dog is behaving badly, are you giving him enough exercise? Dogs end up frustrated and bored if they don't spend enough time on an energetic walk, meeting other dogs, seeing new places and getting the chance to run around off the leash. Your dog will show his frustration not because he's trying to be naughty but because his needs aren't being met.

When the behaviour is unwanted but hasn't been caused by a failure to meet your dog's needs, then you need to use imaginative ways to discourage it. For example, if you don't want him digging up your favourite bedding plants, provide him with a designated area or a sandbox to dig in. When you see him dig in the permitted place, give him a treat and use the all-important positive reinforcement. Eventually you'll be able to phase out the food treats and use positive words alone.

The Bond of Trust

There's good reason why dogs are called 'man's best friend', or of course 'woman's'! Stories abound of how they can travel thousands of miles to find their owner or have sat guarding their owner's grave. The bond of trust and loyalty is a powerful one.

As we talk about elsewhere in the book (see page 29), a dog's bond with a human is very much like that between a child and parent. If you've taken your child to a birthday party and had to peel them off your leg, you'll know how important it is for them to know you're there so that they have the confidence to join in. Dogs are no different. According to Victoria Stilwell in her book *The Secret Language of Dogs,* 'dogs with high human attachment will actually have more confidence to explore novel situations if someone they know and trust is close by.'

The bond of trust doesn't develop by itself. If you're raising your dog from a puppy it may be easier and quicker to build a bond than if your dog came from a rescue centre and had an unhappy life. Training by itself it not enough, so how can you grow and improve the bond?

If you understand your dog's body language, you are more likely to be able to build a strong bond of trust. Communication is key, so be consistent with your commands and rewards: your dog needs to know what is expected of him to feel secure (establishing clear rules is part of this). Remember that you're his role model, so stay calm and don't let him see you angry. Pay him attention by getting down on his level (whilst respecting his space) and letting him know you love him through play, petting and grooming.

If you're thinking that this all sounds very much like being the parent of a small child, then you're absolutely right!

I let the dog out,
or I let him in, and we
talk some. I let him know
I like him, and he lets me
know he likes me.

KURT VONNEGUT

BODY

Sense

BE AWARE OF YOUR OWN
Body Language

Even though your dog has learned that you respond best to verbal interaction, less well to facial expressions and are completely useless at reading smells, he will still respond strongly to your visual cues and will read a lot into your body language. It's important that you understand the messages you send to him using your body, many of which you may be completely unaware of.

Dogs rely a great deal on body language to navigate social encounters with other dogs and it's exactly the same when they interact with humans. What he dislikes is when you send mixed messages which make him feel confused and anxious. For example, if you want to tell your dog to stop doing something, saying 'No' with a firm voice and a frown, followed up by praise after he obeys is much easier for a dog to understand than if you smile, give him lots of strokes and cuddles whilst saying 'You can't have that, no you can't, give it to me, you're a rascal aren't you?'. The dog will think you're playing a game and may act up even more. Make sure that your instructions and your body language match.

The classic human body language failure occurs when recalling your dog. If this has become a battleground with your dog failing to return on command, you will have experienced plenty of frustration and even anger. Now your dog has learned that he gets told off when he comes back to you. When you call him back he can already sense the welling frustration in your body posture. That's why it's important to stay calm and relaxed and to send out happy signals to your dog as you call him to you. Make sure you give him lots of praise when he comes back.

When you stand up, you appear like a skyscraper to your relatively tiny dog. If you want to put him at ease, get down on his level. This is especially applicable in the recall scenario – crouch down and call your dog, so that he can see that you aren't a physical threat. Also, the next time you do go off on a rant, bear in mind that ignoring unwanted behaviour and rewarding desirable behaviour is the best way to live in harmony with your dog, rather than trying to dominate physically and verbally.

BODY LANGUAGE –
Greeting

Dogs use body position, paw placements and their body movements to communicate with each other, and just like with humans, even a dog's involuntary body language expresses important information about his emotional state and social standing.

The body language of greeting is instantly recognizable and proves that dogs are sophisticated pack animals with a social hierarchy. As a general rule, the more dominant the dog, the larger it makes itself appear to be. Submissive, frightened or low-status dogs make themselves look as small and nonthreatening as possible.

When two dogs greet each other, one of them may adopt a stiff-legged upright posture that expresses its dominance. The other dog may break off eye-contact first, lie down or perform a play bow, both of which indicate an acceptance of the other dog's higher status. Dogs then sniff each other's faces, mouths and necks before moving on to the hindquarters. It's an important ritual as well as a quick way of catching up on each other's health and well-being without resorting to small talk. Raised tails is another sign that all is well.

When two dogs of roughly equal status meet, at first they might both appear stiff-legged and upright. Then they may break eye contact and sniff each other's backsides as they stand flank-to-flank, putting both dogs in a potentially vulnerable position, which signals that they are not a threat. Scent reveals further social-ranking information to support the body language (as well as revealing gender, health, emotional state and sexual availability).

If one of the dogs braces its feet, with its body and head sloped forward with ears erect, it is a sign that he doesn't accept the other dog as sharing equal status and is willing to fight to assert dominance. The other dog might decide to stand or sit still, submitting to allow the dominant dog to approach and sniff its hindquarters, and thus avoid physical conflict. If a strange dog approaches you with hackles raised and you sense a potential conflict, some experts recommend de-escalating the situation by telling your dog to sit.

BODY LANGUAGE –

Expressing Dominance

As we saw in the previous section, greeting dogs signal their social status using body language. There are several other ways that dogs express their dominance which you should also look out for. The easiest to read is when a dominant dog stands over a submissive dog that is lying down. You see this behaviour frequently with adult dogs over puppies.

Another common display of dominance is when one dog places its head or paw on the shoulder of the other, once again physically dominating the other dog with its height. Sometimes a confident dog will even go so far as to shoulder bump another dog to express its dominance, after bounding up for a greeting at speed, even knocking the other dog off balance.

Leaning on another dog has been interpreted by many experts as a less rambunctious form of the shoulder barge. The dominant dog simply positions itself close to the other dog and then leans against it, which will make the other dog move away slightly. Sometimes this body language is so subtle that it can be difficult to spot because the physical movements have been reduced to the point of being symbolic and ritualistic rather than functional.

Your dog will try some of these moves on you when you're sharing a bed or sofa. Even though this behaviour is hilarious, don't budge an inch. You're the boss. Gently pull him down to your level or sit up so that you are higher, otherwise you'll end up literally fighting for bed space (some dogs are allowed to dominate so often by oblivious owners that eventually they find they can't get into bed without being growled at).

Also look out for when two dogs make a T-shape, where the lower-ranking dog turns its flank towards the other, so that the dominant dog's head is on or close to its back. Alternatively, the lower-ranking dog may avoid a confrontation by sniffing the ground, which means the other dog can no longer say with his body language, 'What do think you're looking at?'. Humans do this too with averted gaze. Aggressive humans hate being stared at and will often start a fight if they think others are disrespecting them by maintaining eye contact. Look away or become preoccupied with something else and the bully can't escalate the conflict without looking stupid.

BODY LANGUAGE –
Relaxed and Happy

It's fairly easy to read the body language of a happy dog. We've co-existed for thousands of years so there's been plenty of time for some dog expressions to come close to mimicking those of humans. If your dog looks like he's smiling – mouth open, tongue sticking out a bit or lolling over the lower teeth, edge of the lips curled upwards – he probably is.

Happy dogs hold their heads in a neutral position (neither thrust forward or turned anxiously away), the ears are also relaxed and without tension. The face and eyes look relaxed – blinking is a sign of relaxation and dogs often blink to calm themselves – and the tail may be wagging gently from side to side.

There's nothing more rewarding than watching a happy dog going about his business with his tail wagging rhythmically like the doggy equivalent of humming. Sleepy dogs seem pretty contented too, although if your dog is overdue a walk it's easy to interpret this as boredom or your dog just killing time until you say 'walkies'. However, in general, a sleepy dog is comfortable and happy. He may curl up into a ball (especially if it's cold) or if he's feeling super relaxed, stretch out and lie on his back, exposing his belly. When a dog does a belly roll, like a cat he is showing complete trust and submission, but unlike a cat he is probably inviting you to rub his belly. Wolf puppies have their bellies licked by their mothers to make them go to the toilet, so some experts claim that dogs love belly rubs because of ancestral memories of maternal comfort. Or maybe it's just because belly rubs are fun and great for bonding; dogs love having them and humans love giving them.

Dogs are social animals and like nothing better than to be with us. This is even apparent at a biochemical level. Tests have shown that levels of the hormone oxytocin – the hormone connected to social bonding and which the human body releases when we are in love – rise in dogs after they have been petted by their owners. So, if you want a happy dog, give him lots of company and attention (as well as plenty of exercise and a well-balanced diet). It's really that simple. Dogs are happy if they are given all the things that they need.

BODY LANGUAGE –

Anxious and Stressed

Dogs can express stress in as many and varied ways as humans do, mainly through body language but also behaviour. Anxious body language is easy to spot: the dog's body gestures are slow and cautious, the tail is lowered and may be tucked beneath the legs, the ears are pushed back flat against the head, the mouth is closed and tense, or else the dog may be panting excessively and/ or licking his lips. As anxiety turns into fear, this body language will develop further (see page 48).

Another common sign of anxiety is raising the front paw – a curtailed version of a bigger sign of submission. When a dog rolls onto his back in submission, he begins by raising the front paw and then rolling the front part of his body. Raising the paw is the first part of this procedure, so it expresses anxiety and uncertainty.

Your dog will also look to you for guidance and reassurance when he is feeling anxious, in the same way that a toddler scans a parent's face for clues about how to react to a strange situation. You can reassure your dog by staying calm, smiling and saying relaxing phrases in a soothing voice: 'It's fine, everything's OK'. When meeting a strange dog, encourage the two dogs to make friends and take the lead by allowing the other dog to sniff your outstretched hand. Use your judgement though. If the other dog looks frightened and aggressive, avoid eye contact, stand still and stay calm. Don't run away or start shouting as this will increase the stress for everyone and increase the chances of an attack. Usually tensions are resolved after both dogs have had a mutual sniff.

Persistent anxiety is also easy to spot and treatable (usually by changing your behaviour). For example, your dog may express his separation anxiety when you leave the house by barking and howling incessantly, causing damage with his teeth and claws, going to the toilet and even by self-harming. You can begin by encouraging the dog to spend time alone in another room whilst you are still in the house, then reward him with praise and a treat. Then start leaving him alone for short periods and always give fuss and a treat on your return so that he begins to associate your leaving with the anticipation of your inevitable happy return.

BODY LANGUAGE –
Anger and Fear

When dogs are scared or angry, their body language presents the same. Expressed as defensive aggression, this body language is designed to prevent what neither dog really wants – a full on physical fight. However, a scared or angry dog may exhibit appeasement as the first line of defence and then move onto aggressive behaviour after the appeasement has failed.

In submissive/appeasement mode, the ears are pulled tightly back against the head, the dog sits, cowers (legs bent, hindquarters low, head withdrawn or in line with the lowered body) or lies down and rolls over in complete submission. In extremis, he may also urinate, like a puppy, in abject appeasement. Other fear responses include raised hackles, completely freezing on the spot, hiding, pacing or spinning (displacement activities designed to work off some adrenalin and self-calm), yawning, lip licking, drooling, trembling, rapid panting and self-directed chewing (most commonly of paws and flank).

Another common expression of fear is when the dog turns his head away but keeps his eyes fixed on the perceived threat, so the whites of his eyes are visible (this is called 'whale eye'). The tail is often held between the legs, but it may be high over the back with the hair puffed out.

In preparation-for-attack mode, the ears are rotated sharply forward, the dog bares his teeth, the body is held tight and rigid with stiff, locked legs, he may lunge forward, eyes either locked onto the other dog or staring into space. He may growl, which develops into snarling and snapping, with lips drawn back from the teeth. At this stage, biting is imminent.

Even when a dog attacks, his main motivation is to make the perceived threat go away, not to inflict maximum harm. A dog will usually only attack when he feels cornered and that he has no other choice. It's important to recognize the warning signs of anger and fear, so that this extreme measure can be avoided. For example, a yawning dog appears harmless on the surface, but when combined with some of the other physical expressions of fear, a yawn should be interpreted as a warning. Likewise, a wagging tail does not communicate happiness and contentment in the context of fear arousal.

BODY LANGUAGE –

Playing

Dogs have quite a limited repertoire of games, namely: running, chasing, play fighting and wrestling and tug of war. These games are vitally important for a puppy's development and bonding with its pack of humans and other family dogs, socialising with unfamiliar dogs, as well as having fun in adulthood and making new friends.

Dogs never seem to tire of playing the same old games and they can switch games in the blink of an eye; chase me can tumble into a roll-about play fight and then back into 'bet-you-can't-get-my-ball' within a few seconds. Another favourite is what we would call 'chicken', where one dog runs full pelt at the other one, then veers off at the last minute. Hide-and-seek and 'fetch' are popular dog–human games.

Dogs invite each other to play with a play bow – crouching with the front legs straight, hindquarters and tail stuck high in the air, with optional bouncing if very excited, or if the other dog doesn't respond. Then it's straight into high octane romping, dashing, chewing, chasing play. Sometimes you might see your dog bound enthusiastically up to another at full pelt (tail whirling confidently in a big circle), then stop dead and do a play bow just at the moment when you think they are going to collide. This mock attack is all part of the invitation to play. Sometimes you might see an adult dog roll onto its back in full passive display in order to cajole a more timid dog or puppy into playing. He may even paw at the puppy from this supine position.

Sometimes if play gets too frenetic or rough, one of the dogs will perform a quick play bow just to remind everyone that it's all in good fun and no harm meant. Puppies quickly learn acceptable boundaries whilst playing. If they bite a littermate too hard, they'll hear a yelp and play stops. You can do the same when your puppy's sharp little teeth hurt you, by letting out a deliberate little yelp and then stopping the game for a while. Your puppy will soon be all over you with apologetic licks.

BODY LANGUAGE –
Frustrated and Bored

Frustration is really just another word for stress. It is caused by the inability to satisfy a need or desire and can be the cause of so-called 'problem behaviour'. If your dog seems grumpy, has unpredictable moods and behaviour, is digging or urinating in the 'wrong' place or keeps defying your best training efforts, you have a frustrated and bored dog. All these 'bad' behaviours are a signal that one or more of his needs or desires are not being met. It's your job to figure out what is lacking and make the necessary changes.

Signs that your dog is frustrated and bored include destructive behaviour (that poor couch), digging, chasing his tail, demand barking, pacing, whining and listlessness. These are all behaviours that either help him to self-calm or demand your attention.

Plentiful exercise is essential to stop your dog getting bored. It's not just the quantity of exercise that makes life fun for them, it's also the opportunity to see new places, meet people and other animals, and run free off the leash. So, keep your dog's walks varied and make his life more interesting. Just think how bored and frustrated you get on the same old daily commute!

If your dog is home alone then he might experience 'isolation distress'. This is a reaction to the stress and anxiety caused by his favourite person – you – not being home (even though he knows you always come back). If you come home to shredded cushions or raided bins, this isn't your dog being naughty, he's just expressing his frustration at being by himself. Try to build up the time apart from him so that he gets used to it gradually. Leaving a radio on when you're out can be soothing.

Always come back to basics. Are you keeping your dog physically and mentally stimulated? If you're not maintaining your side of the agreement/social contract with him, he has every right to vent his frustration.

Jumping Up

It is common for dogs, especially puppies, to jump up on you with their front paws when you return home. With little dogs this isn't a big problem, unless you don't like it and want it to stop; with bigger dogs it might not bother you, but it should be discouraged as it could be dangerous for him to jump up on a frail old person, a child, or a grumpy friend.

Regardless, it's your responsibility to manage the behaviour and you do owe your fellow humans the common courtesy of not being knocked over or covered in mud by your beloved hound.

Dogs jump on us because they want to get their face as close to our faces as possible. If you crouch down so that your faces are closer, you're not solving the jumping problem. Some experts advise you to gently but firmly put your dog's front paws on the ground, say 'down' and then ignore him until he's calmed down. It is better to turn your back and take away your attention completely, then you can praise him when he's calmer and has stopped jumping on you. Whenever you think a dog is about to jump on you in friendship, turning your back nearly always stops the dog from jumping, and if not, at least he can't land both paws painfully on your stomach.

If you ignore a jumping dog, he will quickly learn that he only gets praise and attention when he has four feet on the ground. Whatever you decide, everyone in the household must be consistent. Either you decide that you don't mind your dog jumping up (and you must face the consequences of him jumping on strangers); or you make it a rule that he is never rewarded for jumping up. If it's one rule for you and another for strangers, your dog will become anxious and confused, which isn't fair.

Consistency is vital when it comes to any rules of the house. If you allow your dog to jump on the sofa, then you need to make sure everyone else in the household is fine with it; if you feed him from the table, expect him to beg; if you allow him to snatch treats from your hand, he will do the same with children. Make sure everyone is happy to uphold the rules, otherwise you'll be fighting a losing battle!

TAIL
Talk

Dogs use their tails very expressively to convey intent. Dogs of different breeds share a common tail language, although strongly curved tails like the Husky's can be hard to read, as their movements can be more subtle. Tails are great for signalling over long distances, so approaching animals can read the situation whilst still quite far away.

A dog who has had his tail docked is at a distinct social disadvantage in the company of other dogs.

Dogs wag their tails enthusiastically in a broad sweep when a member of the pack returns home or when something exciting is about to happen, such as going for a walk. Here it is an expression of happiness and pleasurable excitement. But a tense tail, wagging high, fast and stiff, can also be a sign of aggression, so look out for other emotional clues to get the whole picture (see page 112). A submissive dog may also wag his tail quickly whilst crouching or cowering.

Generally, when the tail is held high and curls a little over the hindquarters, the dog is feeling happy and confident. This also allows his scent to spread into the air to announce his presence. The tail will adopt a horizontal position if the dog feels unsure or conflicted, and it disappears between the hind legs during moments of high anxiety and fear, or when signalling subordination. However, some breeds like hounds (and especially greyhounds) tend to keep their tails between their legs as a neutral position – that doesn't mean the dog is miserable. Mostly, a relaxed tail (rather than an excited one) is held at 45 degrees to the ground and may stay at this angle during a happy wag.

Experts have even managed to decode the direction of the wag. An uninhibited, happy wag often involves the entire backside and can be described as a helicopter tail – wagging in a circular movement as the dog enthusiastically gambols up to greet. However, dogs tend to wag more to the right when they meet a familiar person or dog (although a confident and sociable dog will wag to the right with a strange dog but will hold the tail lower). They wag more to the left when meeting an unfamiliar dog or something that makes them want to retreat, such as a dog standing aggressively. Dogs also react differently to the left-right orientation of the tails of other dogs.

Canine
Facial Expressions

Learning what your dog's facial expressions mean is invaluable if you combine it with your knowledge of her body language. Dogs have facial expressions that they only use with humans (see page 20), demonstrating our unique, long-standing bond. In fact, facial expressions are the one language that humans and dogs share.

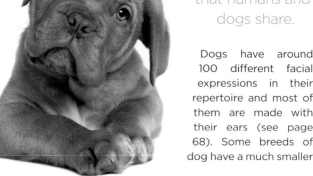

Dogs have around 100 different facial expressions in their repertoire and most of them are made with their ears (see page 68). Some breeds of dog have a much smaller range because of the way they've been bred, for example bulldogs and pitbulls only have 10 expressions. This leaves them at a disadvantage when communicating with other dogs as their faces are easy to misread, causing fights to develop.

Here are some of the most common facial expressions you'll see your dog pulling:

Brows: If your dog is calm and relaxed then she'll have a smooth brow with no wrinkles. Raised eyebrows indicate – you've guessed it – surprise, but can also be a sign that your dog is feeling uncertain about something.

'Puppy dog eyes': By raising their brow, dogs can make their eyes look bigger, like a child's. To humans, it looks like they're crying out for love and care and that's what we'll give them after our hearts have stopped melting. It won't take long for a dog to learn what wonderful rewards this facial expression brings!

Bowed head: Your dog is unsure what reaction they are going to get from you. This is more common in anxious, shy and submissive dogs.

Mouths: Lines around your dog's mouth signify tension. If the area around her mouth is smooth, she's relaxed.

Head tilting: This indicates a focused dog who's ready for the next instruction.

Squinting, half-lidded eyes: Aw. Your dog is in seventh heaven! She's so relaxed she can't even be bothered to open her eyes properly.

'Whale eye': If your dog is looking at you intently from the corner of her eye so that the whites of her eyes are showing, this is 'whale eye'. It's a signal that she's fearful and may be about to respond aggressively. Give her some space.

In order to really enjoy a dog,
one doesn't merely try to
train him to be semi-human.
The point of it is to open
oneself to the possibility of
becoming partly a dog.

EDWARD HOAGLAND

Senses

Eyesight

Sighted humans are driven by what they see and it's their primary way of interpreting the world around them, so it's easy to forget that a dog's eyesight is less important to them than smell and hearing. Alexandra Horowitz, author of *Inside of a Dog*, expresses this perfectly when she says, 'when a dog turns his head toward you, it is not so much to look at you with his eyes; rather, it is to get his nose to look at you. The eyes just come along for the ride.'

A dog's eye is quite similar to a human's in its design and performance, but he only sees in shades of yellow and blue (which is an improvement on the persistent myth that dogs only see in black and white). Experts now believe that a dog's colour perception is akin to a red-green colour-blind human. He also has a translucent third eyelid called the 'nictitating membrane' hidden beneath the lower lid, which can protect against dust and keep the eye moist.

The retina, the light sensitive area inside the eye, is composed of two types of photoreceptors: cones and rods. The cones allow colour vision and high visual acuity (i.e. seeing in detail), while the rods operate at lower light levels but with a lower visual acuity. Dogs have about one quarter of the visual acuity of humans, because humans have a fovea in their retina – a little pit that provides the clearest vision of all – which dogs lack. Instead, dogs have a 'visual streak' which is a line of high-density cells across the back of the retina, which is why dogs often cock their heads when they are focusing intently on something. It's also why a dog can chase after and track a ball at a distance, but at other times can't see a toy that he is practically standing on.

Dogs have bigger pupils and a much higher ratio of rods to cones than humans, so they only need about one fifth of the light we need to see. This is why they can operate so effectively in near darkness (although they can't actually see in the dark). They are 'crepuscular', which means they like to hunt in the dim light of dawn and dusk. Dogs also have a special reflective layer behind the retina called the tapetum lucidum, which reflects light back onto the retina, improving low light vision even further (it's also the reason dogs' eyes glow in the dark). Dogs have better peripheral vision than humans (up to 250 degrees depending on the breed, compared to our 180), because of their lateral placement, but we see more of the colour spectrum.

EYE
Communication

Dogs have large expressive eyes; it's one of the reasons we find them so irresistible. They do use their eyes to express emotions, so look more closely and you can read your dog's emotional state. Eye contact is also a vital part of communication between dogs, which minimizes conflict by reinforcing a social hierarchy.

Dogs will stare intently at something if they are unsure of it, but when two dogs meet, the more submissive dog will avert his gaze, while the dominant dog maintains eye contact. In fact, a particularly submissive dog will go to almost comical lengths to avoid eye contact – for example, by suddenly becoming totally engrossed in a tuft of grass or some other object – to send the message that he is so nonchalant about the presence of the other dog he can't possibly be a threat.

Dogs also blink to appease and display friendly eye contact to tell other dogs, 'I am friendly, I mean no harm.' A blink communicates relaxation and calmness, which reduces anxiety in the other dog and helps to diffuse any tension. By blinking slowly in your dog's presence, you can indicate that you are happy and pose no threat and that you trust him not to attack you while your eyes are closed! When you see your dog lying on the sofa with his eyes half closed, you can be sure that he is content and relaxed.

It's okay to stare lovingly at your dog because he knows you're not a threat (don't try the same with cats though), but it's inadvisable to stare at strange dogs as they may perceive this as aggression. The best way to put strange dogs at their ease (and you will meet many whilst walking your own dog) is to minimize eye contact and approach with your body slightly angled, rather than square on, and talk in a soft voice.

When a dog is excited or interested in something, his pupils dilate and he will fix a stare. When he stares at you intently, begging for food, you would be mistaken if you believed that it is mere arousal – in fact, your dog's stare is an expression of dominance, so when you give him food you are giving him the signal that he is the boss. That alone should be sufficient reason never to feed your dog scraps from your table.

Hearing

A dog's sense of smell ranks first, but they also have amazing hearing. Humans can only hear up to about 20kHz, but a dog can hear frequencies up to 45kHz. That's probably how they hear the mail arriving when it's still two miles down the road! Dogs are born deaf, which is why smell and touch are such important senses in the early days, but it only takes a month for puppies to develop their incredible hearing.

Certain breeds of dog have more sensitive hearing, which can make them prone to anxious behaviour. Bear this is in mind when creating noise around the house, be it your screaming children at play or your weekly vacuum. Studies have shown that introducing dogs to loud noises at an early age can desensitize them and make them less likely to have a fear of noise later in life. Not surprisingly, dogs with flat and hairy ears don't hear as well as dogs with erect ears and less hair.

Even when you think it's quiet, the world is a noisy place for your dog. Because she can hear such high frequencies, her ears will be picking up sounds that are beyond the human range. If the frequency is over 36kHz it can be painful for her and cause whining or barking. Did you know that the Beatles' song 'A Day in the Life' deliberately includes a whistling sound after the last chord of the song that is at a high frequency only dogs can hear?

Can you wiggle your ears? Probably not much. Your dog has over 18 muscles in her ears that allow them to be rotated, tilted, raised and lowered. Being able to move her ears like this allows her to hone in on and locate exactly where a sound is coming from. But it gets even better: your dog can hear with each ear independently. This gives her the ability to listen to two different sounds at once and to filter sounds (one of the reasons dogs are great at search and rescue). Just imagine how useful this would be as a human superpower!

EAR
Position

A dog's ears aren't just for listening, they are used for talking and communicating too. The ear position and shape changes with a dog's mood and circumstances. If her ears are erect and facing forward ('pricked' ears) then she is engaged, interested and ready to listen. If they are also pulled slightly back, then she is feeling friendly. Your dog will also raise her ears up and forward when she's feeling aggressive, so consider her other body language when interpreting this ear position.

When your dog holds her ears in their 'neutral' position – not pricked or pulled back flat on her head – she is feeling relaxed. A relaxed ear position may also be accompanied by an open mouth and drooping tongue.

We know from page 67 that dogs move their ears independently to focus on different sounds. If your dog is flicking her ears about, she may be feeling concerned and is trying to use her hearing to figure out what is going on by scanning all around.

When a dog's ears are pinned back it can have different meanings based on how pinned back they are and other body language. Loosely pinned back ears coupled with a relaxed body show that she is happy and feeling friendly. However, if her ears are pinned back tightly and her body is tense then she may be feeling nervous, fearful or submissive.

DOGS AS
Listeners

If your dog always seems to ignore your commands, you might be surprised to learn that they are actually very good listeners. According to a poll in the US, a third of married women said their pets are better listeners than their husbands!

And now for the science bit: research has shown that dogs process speech in the same way as humans do. Not only are they paying close attention to who is speaking, but also how we say it and what we are saying.

Harnessing their listening skills, dogs are being used in schools to help students with reading. A dog will patiently sit and listen, making a child who is struggling with reading feel more relaxed and confident about reading aloud. And, of course, it makes reading fun. Dogs are also used by schools to help reduce stress – time spent playing with, walking and stroking a dog has been proven to calm students. This is incredibly valuable to children who are struggling with home or learning-related issues.

Best of all? Dogs don't judge. Dogs don't take over the conversation. Dogs don't interrupt. Dogs don't have opinions. No wonder they're man's best friend!

Head Position

Understanding what your dog's head position means is another useful technique for communicating with her. For example, if your dog suddenly whips her head around when you're stroking her, it's a warning that it either hurts or that she's simply not comfortable being touched there. Knowing when to stop doing something is vital to your dog's happiness and the trust between you.

Research has shown that the direction dogs turn their heads corresponds to which side of their brain they're using. So, if your dog turns her head to the right, she is using the right side of her brain, and vice versa. Turning her head to the right tends to be associated with negative emotions such as fear and anxiety. Turning her head to the left indicates the processing of more positive emotions. However, in *The Secret Language of Dogs,* Victoria Stilwell argues that the way your dog tilts her head more likely shows that 'she's trying to work out what you're saying rather than having an emotional reaction to how you're saying it … [I]t's the canine way of saying "Huh?"'.

Stanley Coren, well-known for his expertise on dogs, believes that head tilting is more to do with vision. If your dog tilts her head, she may be doing it to get a better view of your mouth and face as you talk, otherwise her muzzle obstructs her view. We already know that dogs scan faces for information and clues, so it's important that she has clear sight of you.

Whiskers

Dog owners don't often pay much attention to the importance of their pet's whiskers, some even trim them. Stop! Whiskers are a vital part of the way your dog makes sense of the world around them. They help him to navigate safely, including in the dark or dim light, and also protect him.

You'll find the stiff hairs all over your dog's face – on his muzzle, cheeks, lips, chin and above his eyes. With deep set roots, whiskers are surrounded by muscle and erectile tissue and are connected to densely packed nerves, giving them their vital sensory power.

The technical name for your dog's whiskers is 'vibrissae' and, as the name suggests, they're all about vibrations. When anything rubs against these sensitive whiskers, the vibrations stimulate nerves and send a message to his brain about his surroundings. 'Of those areas of the brain that register touch in the dog,' says Stanley Cohen, professor of psychology and canine expert, 'nearly 40 per cent of it is dedicated to the face, with a disproportionately large amount of that dedicated to the regions of the upper jaw where the vibrissae are located.' That's a huge proportion and shows just how important whiskers are.

Your dog's whiskers are highly mobile and can indicate how he is feeling. If his whiskers point forwards then he may be feeling threatened. They can also help your dog to detect imminent danger. Highly sensitive to changes in air current, his whiskers will pick up any movement nearby allowing him to be ready and alert. They're sensitive enough to detect changes in wind speed and direction, plus can identify the presence of large objects by sensing the deflection of air currents.

Dogs aren't like cats, who seem able to pour themselves into any space. Your dog will use his whiskers to judge whether he can fit through or into a space. Think parking sensors! The whiskers above your dog's eyes also play an important safety role. When touched, they trigger a blinking reflex that protects his eyes from being injured. Useful if he's running through undergrowth and branches.

As for cutting your dog's whiskers? Don't. Aside from the possible discomfort to your dog, just imagine the satnav being disabled in your car. But if you do accidentally cut his whiskers, never fear, they will grow back.

Mouth

Dogs, like human babies, love to use their mouths to explore the world. For your dog, her mouth is a great physical way to interact with the world and compensates for the fact that she doesn't have opposable thumbs to pick up or carry objects.

There are many ways in which the shape of your dog's mouth can help you understand how she's feeling. If her mouth is slightly open with the tongue gently hanging out, she is feeling relaxed (think about how you look when you fall asleep on the couch on a Friday night). If your dog is interested and attentive, her mouth will be closed. When she pulls her lips back to show her teeth, treat this as a warning – back off or do something to calm her down. Look at the rest of her body too – a tense mouth and an equally tense body is a sign that your dog isn't happy. To show submission, your dog's mouth will stretch back to reveal her rear teeth.

A big question: can dogs smile? Many dog owners think that, yes, of course their canine best friend can smile! Generally, if your dog is relaxed and she seems to curl her lips into a smile, then she's happy (or at least she's trying to keep you happy). Whether it's something dogs have always done to communicate, or whether it's been learned from humans, it's not clear.

Think of a dog's mouth with its lolling tongue and you can't help think about panting. Generally, if your dog pants, particularly after exercise or in hot weather, she is trying to cool herself down. However, panting can also be a sign that she's stressed; consider what her overall body language is saying and take steps to calm and reassure her if she does seem anxious. Worried that you're boring your dog? Actually, a big, exaggerated yawn is another sign that she could be stressed or feeling aggressive. Again, have a look to see if her other body language confirms this.

Animal behaviour research has found that dogs lick their mouths when they see an angry human face. And you just thought she was hungry! It's yet another sign of how in tune your dog is with your emotions and her ability to engage in dog-human communication.

NOSE AND SENSE

of Smell

Your dog's nose is his most important sense organ. He has around 250 million smell receptors in this nose, compared to 5 million in the human nose – that's quite a difference. And if you want to feel even more inferior, the part of your dog's brain that processes smell is 40 times bigger than yours. They also have a special scent organ in the roof of their mouths called the vomeronasal (or Jacobson's) organ (see page 81). So, wake up and smell the coffee (if you can), your dog has an amazing sense of smell!

Your dog's nostrils are pretty special – with one sniff he can gather all kinds of scents that help him to communicate. Even more impressive is that he can move his nostrils independently and therefore determine the direction a smell is coming from.

Dogs can detect individual human smells (and how they change) and use them not only to identify people but also to smell how we are feeling. For example, our natural flight or fight response releases adrenaline, which is a hormone completely undetectable to the human nose but easy for a dog to spot. Your dog can literally smell your fear.

Dogs' amazing noses have been put to good use to help people with medical conditions (see page 91). They've long been used by enforcement agencies to track humans and to sniff out drugs and other illegal substances. In the military, dogs are experts at detecting explosive devices. Combined with their incredible hearing, dogs' sensitive noses have also earned them a vital role in search and rescue operations.

Dogs use their noses to gather a vast amount of information about the world around them. Spraying (see page 88) is one example of canine data collection using scent. Another is the way dogs like to sniff each other's private parts in greeting. It garners specific information about the other dog in a few seconds, such as gender and even what they like to eat.

That dogs should have a cold, wet nose is something of a myth. Your dog keeps his nose wet by licking it as the moisture helps to intensify smells. If his nose is dry, chances are he's just not licked it recently. So rather than using just his nose as an indicator of health, it's far better to keep an eye out for changes in your dog's overall well-being and behaviour, such as not eating or his toilet habits.

The Flehmen Reaction

It sounds like an advanced Pilates move, but the Flehman Reaction is actually a response shared by many animals in which they curl back their upper lip and inhale through their nostrils. It's a behaviour that's been observed in a wide range of species such as horses, cats, zebras, giraffes, goats, elks, snakes, giant pandas and even hedgehogs.

Does your dog lick the air, flick his tongue and smack his mouth, holding this position for several seconds? He's not gone barking mad, it's his Flehmen reaction to sensing something interesting (often with no detectable odour). It's a remarkable ability that allows dogs to learn stacks of information about their environment. Picking up particles with his tongue, he passes them into his mouth and on to his vomeronasal organ, or Jacobson's organ. The organ is in the roof of your dog's mouth and enables him, in a unique way, to combine taste and smell.

The main purpose of the vomeronasal organ is to detect pheromones, the 'sexy' chemicals that let animals know if the opposite sex is ready for breeding. Think of an invisible dating app for your dog, detecting the age, sex and reproductive status of the local doggy scene. It's an important tool for communicating with and receiving messages from other dogs, and when you're out for a walk you'll see your dog stopping and 'Flehmening' at any interesting scents he discovers.

The name originates from the German 'flehmen', meaning to bare the upper teeth, and also from the Upper Saxon German 'flemmen', which means 'to look spiteful'. The Jacobson's organ is named after the nineteenth century Danish surgeon who was fascinated by the human vomeronasal organ (which, sadly, modern scientists believe has limited function).

Taste

Compared to their other super senses, a dog's sense of taste lets them down. Their other senses are far superior to those of humans, yet when it comes to taste, humans win the prize. The human tongue has 9,000 taste buds compared to just 1,700 in a dog's tongue. Whilst puppies are born with some sense of taste, it doesn't develop completely until they are a few weeks old.

Your dog's taste buds are located on his tongue, the roof of his mouth and the back of his throat. Like us, he can taste sweet, sour, salty and bitter flavours. Dogs aren't particularly fond of salty food, but they do have a sweet tooth. Your dog's sweet taste buds respond to a chemical called furaneol, which is found in many fruits. He's an omnivore, not a carnivore, hence why he still has a taste for fruit and other plant materials.

Interestingly, your dog has special taste buds on the tip of his tongue that focus on water – when your dog next laps from his water bowl, have a look to see how the tip of his tongue curls up as it touches the water. Experts think these specific taste buds have evolved to ensure dogs drink enough water, especially after food that dehydrates them. There's a special organ in the roof of your dog's mouth (see page 81) that enables him to 'taste' smells and this supplements his limited sense of taste. For this reason, he may be more drawn towards stronger smelling foods, canned dog food being an example. In fact, smell rather than taste is more likely to dictate what he eats. If it smells good, he'll try to eat it – whether he's allowed to or not.

Fortunately, your dog has evolved to know that if something tastes bad, it's likely to be harmful or poisonous to him. Some of the treats your dog enjoys – for example, cow hoof chew treats – make a human's stomach turn. But not as much as when your dog munches on the poop of rabbits (and other vegetarian animals)! Such 'treats' are rich in B vitamins and his behaviour may be a sign he's deficient in those essential nutrients.

Rabbit poop aside, dogs' taste buds are evolved to detect and enjoy meat, reflecting how in the wild around 80% of their diet would consist of meat. And that's why a roasted joint is never safe left unattended with a dog nearby!

Licking

Licking is an incredibly important part of a dog's life. You could call it a lifesaver: immediately after a puppy is born its mother will lick it to stimulate breathing and movement. The mother's lick is a caress and practical cleaning tool all in one, even helping her puppies to eliminate waste.

In return, puppies will lick their mother's mouth to signal submission. This also stimulates the mother to regurgitate food – a throwback to the behaviour of dogs' ancestors where a mother would bring food home to the den in her stomach rather than drag it.

Licking as a gesture of submission continues into adulthood. Your dog may lick another dog to signal deference, getting herself out of a tight spot with a 'higher ranking' canine acquaintance. It's a useful communication tool by which your dog can let another dog know she's aware of her social status and who's the 'top dog'.

When it comes to licking humans, what is your dog trying to tell you? When and what she licks will tell you a lot about how she's feeling. By smothering you with 'kisses' when you return home, she's communicating joy and telling you how much she loves you. Licking releases stress-relieving, 'feel good' endorphins that induce feelings of pleasure and comfort in your dog. It's also an acknowledgement that you're the boss. As the boss, she's asking you to look after her, for example by feeding her. Don't worry – that doesn't make for selfish licks, it's another confirmation that she loves you and trusts you to take care of her. Your dog might also lick you when she's feeling anxious, again signalling that she needs you to make her feel secure. Sometimes, she'll just want to lick you because you smell or taste nice and she's exploring her environment with her senses. Of course, if you're rewarding licks with food or tummy rubs then your dog will quickly learn that something good comes out of slobbering on you!

We've all heard the expression 'to lick your wounds', meaning to recover your strength and confidence. Wound licking is an instinctive behaviour shared by humans and many other animals, including dogs. When your dog is wounded or has a pain, she will lick the area both to clean it and to lessen the discomfort. Saliva does have healing properties, but it also contains bacteria that can cause a wound to become infected. Make sure any wounds are treated properly so that they don't deteriorate.

Touch

Touch is an incredibly important sense for dogs from the moment they are born. Along with smell and taste, touch is one of the three senses that puppies have at birth. It's all important for nuzzling up to their mother to stimulate her milk flow, particularly as puppies are born blind and deaf. Cuddling up to his mother and littermates is a source of great comfort to a puppy in the early stages of his life. Dogs then transfer that intimacy to their owners and a new social bond is created.

Dogs are pack animals, so their sense of touch is a big part of being social. It not only builds the sense of security from being part of a pack but is also a means of communication. Naturally, as his pack family, your dog will replicate this behaviour with you. Whilst a dog sitting on your lap isn't always convenient (especially if he obstructs your view of your favourite TV show), remember that it's his way of showing he's part of the pack and provides him with comfort and happiness.

You might notice that your dog sometimes 'leans in' to you or other dogs. He will tend to do this if he's feeling anxious as the weight of the touch helps him feel secure. We know how in tune dogs are with humans so if he leans on you it might be because he senses that you are stressed and wants to comfort you. Dogs are wonderful creatures!

Your dog's whiskers (see page 74) play a huge part in how he explores and makes sense of his world. He also has five different types of touch receptors in his skin that respond to different kinds of touch: movement and position, pain, pressure, temperature and chemical stimulation. Even though dogs are highly sensitive to touch, they actually have quite a high pain threshold.

One of the most sensitive areas of your dog is his paws (and he won't thank you for messing with them). The nerve endings in his paws identify the surface and terrain he's moving on and send messages to your dog's brain so he can adapt his movements accordingly. He'll also use his paws to get your attention. If he 'paws' at you then look at his other body language: if he's relaxed and his tail is a-waggin' then he's telling you with his paws that he wants to play; if he's whining and pawing then he's begging for attention.

Most dogs love nuzzling up to their human family and it plays a vital part in the bonding process (see page 16). Your dog's sense of touch is just as important to him as it is to us. If you understand how he uses touch to communicate and how your touch can benefit him, then you have the foundations of a very happy pack.

Spraying

Spraying. Not the nicest word to describe 'scent marking' but an important part of dog communication! Using urine and faeces, it's one of the ways that your dog will mark her territory and leave behind all-important messages and information for other dogs who pass by. A completely normal behaviour (although not always in appropriate places) that thankfully humans don't share!

When a male dog lifts his leg to urinate, it's not just convenient, it's a way of spreading his pee as high and as wide as possible. What this says to other dogs is 'look how big I am!', even if your dog is a tiny chihuahua. Female dogs will also attempt to spray their urine as high as possible; it's not quite so easy for females but they'll give it a very good try! Aside from making themselves appear bigger than they are, the higher and wider your dog can spray her scent, the more likely it is that another dog will pick up the message. If you see your dog scraping at the ground after she's sprayed, she's cleverly wafting the scent up into the air to spread the message even further.

There can be social triggers for spraying. If your dog is experiencing anxiety, she may spray more. It could be that she's worried about a new person in the house, another pet or a new environment. Perhaps she is overexcited or overstimulated. In both these instances, helping your dog to feel calm and secure will hopefully lessen the urine marking.

When you're walking your dog, give her plenty of time to peruse the smells around her. She's gathering lots of information from other dogs. Likewise, don't rush her if she's stopping to spray here, there and everywhere. It's the equivalent of someone wrestling your smartphone from you as you try to send a text message or check Facebook! Males dogs generally spray more than females, but female dogs will spray more when they're in heat to indicate their availability.

Whilst spraying is all well and good when you're out on a walk, if it happens in the home then it's a problem. It can happen for several reasons, including bad training and dominance issues, and even if your dog is house trained. First of all, get your vet to check that it's not being caused by an illness such as a bladder infection. Having ruled illness out, has your dog been spayed or neutered? If she hasn't then she'll tend to be more territorial, hence the marking in the house. Are you giving your dog enough toilet breaks? It could be that she just can't hold it in for as long as you're expecting her to. If your dog has been spraying in the home, buy a special pet cleaner that will eliminate the proteins in the urine that re-attract her to the same spot.

SIXTH

Sense

Dogs, and many other animals, have been revered and feared over the centuries for their ability to foretell an earthquake, volcano eruption or other natural disaster, and more recently for their ability to detect illness in humans. Many pet owners would say that their animal has an uncanny ability to sense certain things, whether it be a storm on the way or a member of the family feeling unhappy. Undoubtedly, dogs are wonderfully in tune with humans and the natural world, but is this really a mysterious sixth sense?

Rather than possessing an extra sense, it is far more likely that it's her existing senses that give your dog her superpowers. Her hearing, sight and sense of smell are so superior to ours that it's no surprise she's one step ahead. One example is earthquakes, where dogs have been known to behave strangely before an earthquake happens. This can be attributed to a dog's ability to hear high frequency sounds and therefore possibly detect shifting ground long before the earthquake itself happens. It's not proven but is a more plausible explanation than psychic ability.

Much the same applies with your dog's uncanny knack of knowing there's a storm on the way. She can smell the rain in the air, sense the drop in air pressure and feel the vibrations of the storm. Humans are also attuned to detecting a storm, but the signs aren't as amplified by their (inferior) senses as a dog's senses are.

Your dog can't tell the time, yet she knows exactly when you're coming home and waits at the door. Don't be spooked out. Her superior hearing means she can detect you're approaching far better than we could (unless you've got a gravel path, you might not hear a visitor until they knock on the door). Her internal clock tells her when something should be happening – just think how she lets you know when it's time for a walk.

We already know how clever dogs' noses are (page 78), but did you know they can detect medical conditions? 'Seizure alert and response' dogs, for example, can detect if a person is about to have an epileptic seizure and warn them. Dogs can also warn people with diabetes if their blood sugar levels are dropping to dangerous levels by detecting a change in the scent of the person's breath. We already knew it of course, but dogs are indeed extraordinary.

To his dog, every man is Napoleon; hence the constant popularity of dogs.

ALDOUS HUXLEY

I'M

Listening

A REPERTOIRE OF

Barks

Dogs have a repertoire of barks for every occasion. Understanding your dog's barks is vital for interpreting what she wants and how she's feeling and to enabling to meet all her emotional and physical needs. You'll soon learn her language and use it to build a strong mutual bond. A word of warning though: your dog has learned from experience (i.e. through you!) that vocalization gets results and she'll use that to her advantage if you let her. Remember who's in charge!

It's not always straightforward to distinguish between different types of barks. You'll notice that the pitch of your dog's bark changes depending on the situation, in the same way a human's tone of voice reveals how they're feeling. The bark you hear when you're playing with her or when you arrive home will be far less intense than the bark she reserves for a stranger encroaching on her territory.

There's a bark for 'let me out', another for 'help!', and more for 'I'm hungry', 'I missed you' or 'I'm stressed'. Barks also ask questions, for example 'where are you?' and 'who are you?'. As you learn to understand your dog, you'll tune in to the different pitch of each bark. You'll also notice that the frequency changes, for example greetings consist of a couple of short barks, whereas a warning will be a burst of several barks.

Barking is an important communication tool, but there are instances when it can become excessive and annoying. For example, if your dog is left outside for a period of time, she may bark repeatedly to signal her loneliness and stress. If you want to stay on good terms with your neighbours, this behaviour needs to be discouraged before it becomes an established habit. It's also not unusual for a dog to fixate on random targets, such as passing bicycles. Not only is it tiresome for you when you're out and about, but it can give the cyclist a fright!

Whilst accepting your dog's need to vocalize to communicate, excessive and unnecessary barking does need to be curbed. It will take time (especially if you've allowed it to become a bad habit) but the longer you leave it the harder it will be to stop. Speak quietly and calmly to your dog – shouting will only make it worse as she'll think you're joining in. Never reward her whilst she's barking; save the reward for when's she stopped, that way she'll learn that responding to the command to be quiet brings good things.

GREETING
Sounds

When you return home and are met by an excited whirlwind of fur and tail, you probably don't get the chance to stop and listen to the sounds your dog is greeting you with. Like humans, dogs have several vocalizations and physical behaviours that they use to welcome people and fellow dogs. When you've got paws and can't shake someone's hand, what you say (or your bark) is all-important.

Meeting you, someone she's familiar with, your dog's most common greeting will be a couple of short, happy barks at a mid to high pitch. These say 'hello!' and precede her usual mad racing around and fussing. If she's really excited to see you then she may whimper (a sign of submission) whilst bouncing around like she's on a pogo stick. And if she's really, really excited, you may hear her teeth chattering in the same way humans' teeth chatter when they're cold. This is a sign that she's absolutely overwhelmed with anticipation – if that doesn't make you feel wanted, what does?!

When she's meeting and greeting strangers, several rapid barks mark an alarm call that once upon a time would have summoned the rest of the pack to attention. What your dog is doing is making you aware that there's someone or something that she doesn't recognize and that it needs dealing with. She's saying: 'I've come across something new and I don't know yet whether it's good or bad. Be ready to help.'

Sometimes your dog's way of greeting people can be a bit too much, particularly if it involves excessive barking and jumping. Dog trainers call this a 'greeting disorder'. Thankfully, it is a habit you can resolve by training your dog to curb the excitement triggering the behaviour. Experts suggest ignoring your dog when they greet you inappropriately, thereby not rewarding their behaviour in any way. Walking away from your dog communicates with her in exactly the same way another dog would do in the wild if faced with too much noise and exuberance. She certainly won't be upset or offended by your snub in the way a human might be.

Growling

Growling is how your dog expresses his irritation and aggression and warns you that you're making him feel nervous and uncomfortable. You should consider it a warning – he's not necessarily about to bite you but he is communicating that you should either move away or stop doing whatever it is that's upsetting him.

Dogs also growl when they're playing or excited. Don't be concerned if your dog growls while playing with another dog but do check out the accompanying body language. A growling dog with a relaxed body is simply being expressive without communicating aggression. However, if you see

that your dog's body is tense and the growling escalates, it's a wise idea to separate him from his playmate in case it turns into a fight.

If your dog growls gently when you're playing with him, he's telling you that he's having fun. There could, however, be a point where it turns into aggression and you need to keep an eye out for that, for example when he's playing with another dog. If your dog's growling becomes more threatening and he snaps at you, it's most definitely time to stop the game. The fun's over.

Does your dog growl when you try to take his favourite ball away from him? This is called 'possession aggression'. (Some humans have it too!) He's telling you that he has no intention of sharing with you and you should back off. Your dog is also possessive of his territory. A growl warns an unwanted visitor that they're encroaching on your dog's property and that he'll defend it if he must. No wonder dogs have such a bad reputation with mailmen!

Experiencing pain can cause your dog to growl. It's not so much an expression of the pain itself as a response to people interfering. We know how uncomfortable it is to be poked and prodded when you're in pain, even if it's a doctor doing it for our own good. Your dog will vocalize his discomfort to the vet with a growl, especially if he's had similar experiences before and associates a trip to the vets with unpleasant emotional and physical feelings.

It's never a good idea to punish your dog for growling, even though it can be unnerving and awkward in certain situations, for example when people are visiting your home. If you teach your dog not to growl, you'll be removing that crucial warning stage, which risks him skipping straight to the biting stage to communicate his annoyance.

Howling

Hear the word 'howl' and you probably think of a wolf howling at the Moon. You'd be right to not immediately think of dogs. Whilst domestic dogs can howl, they do so far less than their ancestors. Wolves and wild dogs howl to signal that the pack should get together or to announce where the boundaries of their territories are. It's not that your dog is choosing not to howl, it just that she has less reason or need to communicate in this way.

Whether or not she uses it, howling is one of your dog's many means of vocal communication. It is a way to attract attention and to contact other dogs. Think of the 'Twilight Bark' scene in *101 Dalmatians,* where Pongo sets off a chain of howling dogs across London to spread the word that the puppies have been stolen. In reality, although some breeds of dog are more likely to howl, for example Malamutes and Beagles, most domestic dogs simply bark if they want attention.

The sound of a howl is a lonely, mournful one. If your dog is experiencing separation or isolation anxiety, then howling is one way of telling the world she's alone and feeling worried. This type of howling arises when your dog is left alone or is separated from you, her pack leader. Such anxiety is normally accompanied by other indicators of stress, for example pacing or being destructive, so if your dog is howling consider what else her body language is telling you.

Howling can also be used by dogs to communicate that they're in physical pain. It's your dog's way of saying 'I'm hurting and it's making me miserable'. Like all dog communication, howling needs to be interpreted in the context in which it's happening. If your dog doesn't normally howl and there are other signs that she's not herself – or, of course, obvious injuries – then get her checked over by a vet. Don't ignore what she's trying to tell you; it's better to err on the side of caution.

Does your dog howl when you sing? Don't be offended, she's most likely prompted by the pitch of your voice. High-pitched sounds, such as emergency vehicles and some musical instruments, will make your dog release her inner wolf and howl. If you have other dogs in the house, expect them all to join in the chorus as a pack. It's their way of feeling like they belong. Or maybe they just enjoy a good singalong! Either way, dogs' howls are perfect for power ballads.

Whining

Whining, whether it be human or animal, can be annoying. (How many times have you told your children to 'stop whining'?) Unlike with humans, where it is both annoying and unnecessary, whining is a crucial communication tool for dogs. Puppies will whine to get attention and to ask for something they need, such as food or simply a nuzzle from their mother. As your dog develops, whining becomes one of the most versatile tools in his communication toolbox.

Stress is one of the most common reasons for your dog to whine. It signals that he has gone beyond his comfort zone, particularly if he's also exhibiting other behaviours associated with stress. Perhaps you're trying to lead him into a new place or have been training him too hard; if he whines then he's not happy and it's your cue to respond in a way that will calm him down and make him feel comfortable again.

Puppies are the biggest whiners. Leave the room and your puppy will whine to demand your attention and immediate return. This is your opportunity to stop such behaviour becoming a bad habit in later life – so take it! If you return to your puppy and give him attention, he'll quickly learn that his whining earns him a reward. What's his incentive to stop? Only reward your dog for quiet behaviour and he'll learn what's expected of him.

As with howling (see page 100) and growling (see page 98), whining can also be a sign that your dog is in pain. It's much like the way humans wince in pain. You may notice that your dog whines when he puts weight on one of his legs or when he sits down, for example – a sure sign that you need to get him to the vets.

Interestingly, whining isn't always used by your dog to demand attention or convey negative feelings. One of the easiest to recognize whines is the excitement whine. If it's accompanied by wiggling, jumping and vigorous tail wagging – pretty much your dog going absolutely loopy and losing control of his emotions – then you have one very excited dog on your hands. If only adult humans still did this! Roll out some of your best calming strategies and with any luck the whining will stop.

On the other end of the spectrum – and proving just how versatile it is – whining can also signal boredom. Dogs are very stubborn, but don't give in and reward this behaviour or you'll be making a rod for your own back. Make sure he has plenty of stimulation and there will be no cause for boredom whining.

Who said communicating with your dog and meeting his many needs would be easy?!

Dogs do speak, but only to those who know how to listen.

ORHAN PAMUK

GROWING

Together

DO DOGS FEEL *Guilty?*

It's very tempting to transfer human characteristics onto dogs, after all they've been by our side for thousands of years. But what about guilt? Is that droopy-eyed look your dog gives you after she's stolen the Christmas joint truly one of repentance? Dog owners certainly seem to think so, but they could be barking up the wrong tree.

Research at the University of Cambridge in the UK suggests that the 'guilty look' isn't your dog expressing remorse but rather her reaction to negative emotions, such as anger or disappointment, that you are displaying through your tone of voice and gestures. The results showed that dogs don't look 'guilty' unless they are being told off. (Unless of course they're clever enough to hide their guilt at other times!) It seems that your dog's guilty face is an expression of a much less complex emotion – fear.

We know that dogs are capable of basic emotions, such as happiness, fear and excitement, but it's not clear whether they experience more complex social emotions, such as guilt or jealousy. Science tell us that dogs' brains are similar to those of animals known to express a guilty conscience, suggesting guilt may be possible – we just don't know for sure if they use that ability. And without being able to ask them, perhaps we'll never know.

THE BEST AND WORST PLACES
to Touch

It is important for a puppy's socialization that she is handled regularly from an early age. This will help her learn to feel secure with human contact and that no part of her body is out of bounds. However, even with the best bonding and grooming sessions (see page 118), she has areas of her body that are more sensitive or are more vulnerable to touch than others. Learn where they are and respect her sensitivities. How you pet your dog can make you their very best friend or the person they steer clear of!

When petting a dog, most people go straight for the traditional head pat. Actually, dogs aren't too keen on having a hand loom over their head, especially if they don't know you. (Imagine if someone did that to you!) However, they do love to be touched on the back of their neck, under their collar and on their shoulders and chest. In the same way that you probably have a favourite part of a massage, individual dogs have their own specific spots where they love to be petted. Your dog may melt into the floor with a firm scratch under her chin, whereas her Boxer pal from the park goes wild for a scratch at the base of his tail.

Reflexes are a wonderful thing and none more so than the one that makes your dog's leg shake involuntarily. Almost all dogs do this and the spot to scratch tends to be on their belly or flanks. The button you've hit is called a scratch reflex and is designed to help your dog get rid of annoyances, for example a pesky fly. You may see a puzzled look on your dog's face – it's a completely involuntary reaction so she'll wonder what on earth is going on!

The areas where most dogs prefer not to be touched are the top of their head, muzzle, ears, legs and paws. Studies have shown that these areas elicit negative responses so are best avoided if you want to stay on best terms with your pet. It's important to teach children where not to touch your dog (or indeed someone else's dog); as friendly as most dogs are, there's still a chance they may react badly. Concentrate on the areas where your dog loves to be scratched and she'll reward you with love and trust. You'll feel both your stress levels drop.

Of course, dogs will put up with much more from someone they are familiar with, but this doesn't mean they enjoy it, they simply tolerate it better!

SO WHY DOES HE ROLL OVER ON His Back?

Dogs do like to fling themselves around and rolling over on their backs is a favourite. (Although it's not your favourite if they happen to have found a muddy puddle or fox poop to writhe in.) Is rolling over something your dog does for fun or does it have other meanings? As with many doggy behaviours, rolling needs to be interpreted in context.

Your dog, although long domesticated, has a primal urge to survive in the wild. One survival tactic is to disguise his own scent – and so back to the fox poop if we can bear it. By rolling in something – the smellier the better – he can cover up his own scent and in doing so protect against being tracked or detected by potential predators. The most you can do is train your dog to leave such temptation well alone. But good luck with that!

When your dog is playing with other dogs, it's common to see him roll over on his back. This can be interpreted in different ways. It's long been believed that it shows submission to the other dog in the game, the doggy way of saying 'mercy!'. By showing his vulnerable belly, your dog acknowledges the dominance of the other dog – a throwback to how his wolf ancestors behaved. Submissive rolling tells you that your dog trusts you as his leader and that he's very happy about it. Add in a tummy tickle and your dog will think he's in seventh heaven.

However, some experts argue that if your dog rolls over on his back he isn't being submissive at all. What it provides is a good defensive position from which he can better dodge the other dog and launch his own assault. This makes sense when you consider that dogs don't like being touched in a way that makes them feel restrained. Far better to be on your back with your paws free than pinned face down by an overzealous playmate.

What do you do if you've got an intense itch on your back but can't reach it? If you're a dog, then naturally you'll roll over on to your back and give yourself a satisfying rub on whatever surface you're lying on. Ah, that's better! But if you see your dog doing this rather a lot, do check that the itching is not being caused by fleas, ticks or an allergy.

AGGRESSIVE BEHAVIOURS

Between Dogs

Aggression is a behaviour that needs to be managed and never ignored. It links to predatory, sexual, protective, dominance and territorial behaviours and often indicates that your dog is stressed. When your dog displays aggression, she is giving a warning in the first instance. She doesn't want to get into a full-on fight so by giving that warning, other dogs (or indeed humans) are given the opportunity to step away and give her the space she needs.

Common indicators of aggression include: staring eyes, a tense body, exposed teeth, pricked ears, snapping, tail wagging and growling. If allowed to escalate, the aggression will lead to biting – something you definitely want to avoid. Aggressive behaviour should therefore never be ignored and if you don't manage it then it will continue. Poor socialization is one of the root causes of aggression; if your dog hasn't learnt to interact with other dogs then encountering one can be confusing and stressful for her. She won't understand what is and isn't appropriate behaviour and, in her confusion, will default to aggression.

Muzzles will prevent biting but they are not a solution to the problem. As with many behavioural issues, obedience training is key. Unless your dog sees you as her leader, and a trusted one at that, you will not be able to control her. To instil discipline, she must be prepared to listen to you and obey your commands. If she doesn't, you need to work on strengthening the bond between you so that you win her respect. Never deal with aggression by comforting your dog as this will just teach her that it's a behaviour that gets rewarded with love and attention.

If you have one or more dogs in your home, aggressive behaviour is incredibly stressful for everyone, dog or human. It can range from dogs battling for dominance, to fighting over food, to competing for human attention. Once you've figured out what the trigger is, you can work on the solution. It could be as simple as moving food bowls further apart or removing the favourite chair that your dogs compete for. Less simple but just as effective is ensuring that the dogs respond to your commands so that when you intervene you make an impact. Back to obedience training!

TEN SIGNS OF
Illness

Unless your dog is very lucky, she will get ill at some point in her life. Therefore, it's worth knowing a few signs of illness and their possible causes. The following advice is only an introduction and no substitute for consulting a trained professional. If you have any concerns about the health of your puppy or dog, contact your vet immediately.

LETHARGY OR LACK OF INTEREST

Dogs and puppies spend a lot of time sleeping, but they are also highly active, playful and inquisitive when they are awake. You'll soon get to know what a normal level of activity is for your dog. If she appears to have lost all interest in her surroundings and just wants to sleep, contact your vet.

VOMITING

All dogs vomit every so often and the reason is usually that they've been eating too fast or have eaten something they shouldn't have. However, if they are vomiting frequently over the course of a day and have other symptoms, such as no appetite or blood in their vomit, you need to take them to the vets. Causes include a change in diet, food poisoning, intestinal parasites, liver and kidney problems, foreign objects in the intestines or viral infections.

DIARRHOEA

Diarrhoea is commonly caused by a sudden change of diet. If you run out of dog food and offer a short-term substitute, you can expect your dog to get diarrhoea. But loose stools can be a sign of more serious problems, especially if they continue for more than a day or two, contain blood, or are accompanied by fever or vomiting. If you can't pin it down to a simple change in diet, see your vet.

EXCESSIVE URINATION

If your dog makes several trips to pee without producing any results, starts urinating more frequently or urinating in unusual places, she may have a urinary tract infection or blockage. If the colour of the urine is much darker than normal – deep orange, brown or red instead of the normal yellow – she may be dehydrated or have something more serious such as kidney problems.

GUMS

Dogs gums change colour when they are unwell, so checking your dog's gums is a good way to monitor her health. If you notice that her gums are pale, blue, bright red or yellow, it's a sign that you need to get her checked out by the vet as soon as possible. Causes can include anaemia, diabetes, hypoglycaemia, poor circulation and liver or blood clotting problems.

SIGNS OF POISONING

If your dog is drooling, vomiting, lethargic, has diarrhoea or a loss of appetite, these could be the early signs of poisoning. The symptoms progress with excessive thirst or urination and tell-tale nervousness, muscle twitching or seizures and then coma. As soon as you suspect that your dog has ingested poison, it is imperative that you get treatment as quickly as possible. The vet will need to administer an emetic to induce vomiting, to minimize internal damage, and then sedate her to control life-threatening seizures if the symptoms are well advanced.

PANTING, COUGHING, SNEEZING
AND WHEEZING

When a dog pants or coughs it is usually a sign of overheating or overexertion. Take her somewhere cool and encourage her to stay still and calm down. Putting cold water on the pads of her paws (where her sweat glands are) can help. Sneezing, wheezing or repeated coughing is often the sign of a respiratory tract problem or something else that requires immediate attention, such as kennel cough or heartworms, so don't delay, visit the vet right away.

LOSS OF APPETITE

Like humans, your dog may eat less if she's stressed or getting older. However, loss of appetite can also be a sign of illness, especially in combination with other symptoms. If your dog refuses to eat for more than 24 hours, visit your vet to rule out any serious illnesses such as liver or kidney problems, cancer or infection.

STIFFNESS OR DIFFICULTY IN RISING
OR CLIMBING STAIRS

If your dog has had a recent injury or operation, her movement may be limited. However, if there's no obvious explanation you should seek advice from your vet. Stiffness and lameness can be a sign of arthritis, dysplasia of the hips or ligament problems.

EXCESSIVE SCRATCHING OR HAIR LOSS

Dogs love a good scratch, but you will notice if it becomes more frequent that usual. Excessive scratching can be a sign of fleas, ticks or mites, stress and allergies. These aren't serious but do need to be treated. Visit the vet to make sure it's not something more serious, as itching and hair loss are also caused by fungal and yeast infections and endocrine disorders.

BONDING THROUGH

Grooming

Think 'grooming' and you may have an image of show dogs pimped and pruned like ornamental shrubs. In reality, grooming is a much more mundane part of owning a dog but a great opportunity to spend time and bond with them.

Dogs may be pretty good at self-care but they do still need your help to keep in top condition. Grooming your dog is an important part of helping him to keep clean, and done regularly, can help you spot any changes in his health, such as lumps, scratches and insect bites.

For most mammals, grooming is a social behaviour that cements bonds in a family or pack group. Gentle, confident grooming will build your dog's trust in you, so make sure you know how to do it properly. If you cause discomfort to your dog, then he'll lose trust and start to avoid grooming time altogether. This is exactly what you don't want from an activity that's been scientifically proven to reduce stress and blood pressure in both you and your pooch!

Start grooming when your dog is a puppy and he'll get used to being handled and touched gently and in a positive way. Experts think this can help prevent behavioural issues later in your dog's life, such as aggressive protection of his possessions. The grooming establishes a positive relationship where your dog accepts and trusts you to be the one in control.

- Choose a time when your dog is relaxed, maybe after feeding when he's feeling content and sleepy. Start by using your fingers to loosen any tangles or matted hair.

- Invest in a good comb. Carefully work out any knots. Follow up with a wire brush or a bristle brush to remove dirt and loose hair.

- Groom for up to 10 minutes or for as long as your dog continues to enjoy it. You'll soon learn what your dog does and doesn't like. Afterwards, reward him with a little treat.

How often you groom depends on your dog, their coat type and how much they shed. Long-haired dogs should ideally be groomed every day to prevent tangles developing. Medium coats should get your pampering touch once a week. Short haired dogs can go for longer.

TEACHING
Vocabulary

We already know how smart dogs are (see page 28). They're great listeners and, with specialist training, the cleverest dogs can learn up to 250 words and gestures (around 165 words with basic training). Amazingly, Chaser the Border Collie has a vocabulary of over 1,000 words, more than any other animal or species except humans. Tests showed that she can also understand sentences with multiple grammar components.

That's pretty amazing. Your pet may not be a doggy genius like Chaser (some breeds are more receptive than others) but you can still teach him enough vocabulary to ease communication between the two of you and introduce some fun.

When you're trying to teach new words, positive reinforcement is the golden rule, much the same as with any training. Using positive reinforcement and treats will also make it a fun experience – your dog simply won't learn if he's bored or doesn't understand what you're asking of him.

By naming each of your dog's toys, he can associate a concrete word with objects. If you teach him a word like 'hungry' you may think he is responding to an abstract concept, but really he will learn to associate the word with every time you take a tin of dog food, or his bowl, out of the kitchen cupboard. It's the concrete not the abstract that he's responding to.

When you're teaching new vocabulary, don't overwhelm your dog. Start with one object at a time and repeat, repeat, repeat. And, of course, be consistent (see page 122). The easiest way for him to learn a new word is to attach it to an action, so encourage him to find the named object and bring it to you. Try not to get frustrated if it takes a while for your dog to catch on. If you do get frustrated, he'll hear it in your voice and see it in your gestures and this isn't conducive to learning. It certainly doesn't make it fun!

As with learning anything, teaching your dog new words has the benefit of keeping him mentally challenged and stimulated. The more you can understand each other, the stronger your bond and the happier your relationship.

Consistency is Key

With dogs, consistency is key to successful communication. It is the basis for providing your dog with a familiar routine so that he can feel happy and secure. Dogs become nervous and anxious when there are too many changes to their routine and this can manifest in undesirable behaviours, for example chewing, digging, spraying and excessive licking.

Whilst dogs obviously can't tell the actual time, they do have a very effective internal body clock. Your day doesn't have to be regimented down to the last minute, but if you can manage to do feeding, playing, grooming, walks and other regular activities at roughly the same time, your dog can use these signposts to structure his day. Imagine if you spent every day of your life not knowing when you were going to eat, sleep, take a shower or see your friends. All animals need some routine, otherwise they feel out of control. Establish these routines early on and you're less likely to have problems later.

If you suddenly experience a big change, such as introducing a new family member or pet, or going to work all day rather than staying at home, this will inevitably impact on your dog. It's important to recognize how such changes affect your dog emotionally and to minimize the effects. For example, if you're away from the home, an automatic feeder can ensure he is fed at his usual time.

Be consistent with your intent and expression when communicating with your dog. For example, if you're busy and you don't have time to play with him, say 'later' in a firm tone and turn your body away. Both your verbal and non-verbal cues must be consistent. Don't send mixed messages by stroking him because you feel guilty. This just confuses him and it's no wonder he comes back to disturb you a dozen more times before he gets it.

Lack of consistency creates a poorly trained dog and a frustrated owner. Use a commanding tone (deep, loud and firm but not shouting) when he is doing something that you consider wrong and that you want him to stop. If you want your dog to respect boundaries in your home and when you're out, then you must be consistent. For this to be successful, everyone in the household needs to be on the same page: use the same tones and commands and follow the same rules, otherwise you risk confusing your dog.

TRAINING FOR

Tricks

As we have seen on page 120, dogs can learn a vocabulary of around 250 words. Once your dog has mastered her basic obedience training, why not try teaching her a few tricks? This can be a lot of fun for both of you and provides another way of interacting and bonding with your dog. Tricks will also keep her alert and active.

If you want your dog to be receptive to learning tricks, you need to make it fun for her. The more you praise and reward her, the more likely she is to learn. Only practice the tricks for a few minutes at a time or else you risk boring her. Once she has mastered a trick, you'll still have to repeat the routine again the next day and keep revisiting it regularly so that she doesn't forget what she's learned.

But what about the old adage 'you can't teach an old dog new tricks'? Another myth. In fact, it is easier to teach an adult dog tricks as they can focus for longer than puppies. You might need to accept that an older dog has some physical limitations – she doesn't have the boundless energy of a pup anymore – but with positive reinforcement and patience there's no reason why she can't outperform the young pretenders.

The classic trick we're all familiar with is 'fetch'. It's not a skill that dogs have naturally, and some dogs, depending on their breed, simply can't master it. Try it and see: start with her favourite ball and encourage her to drop it into your hand. When she does, give it straight back to her and repeat until she learns to give the ball to you freely. Then throw the ball a short distance, saying 'fetch' and holding out your palm. Praise your dog and give her a small treat every time she brings you the ball. Gradually extend the distance further and further until – hey presto! – you're both giving David Copperfield a run for his money.

Rolling over is another simple trick that's easy for dogs to learn. Once she's mastered that, up the ante by getting her to hold the pose. And there you have it: 'playing dead'. If you think your dog is happy and ready, move on to more tricks. Other favourites include: spinning, begging, waving, taking a bow, and balancing a biscuit on the end of her nose.

Learning tricks is a great way to keep your dog mentally stimulated. Not everything works, and your dog may sometimes struggle to understand what it is that you want her to do. Be patient, persevere and, most of all, have fun together. Even if you don't make it onto a TV talent show, you'll have had a barrel of laughs and barks in the process!

HOW TO MASSAGE
Your Dog

Dogs love feeling close to their owners so petting and grooming are therefore perfect ways to spend time bonding with each other (see page 118). Properly performed, massage will benefit your dog's health and well-being as well as deepen your special bond. Chances are that you'll lower your own blood pressure as well.

1. Choose a time when your dog is already relaxed, submissive and open to being handled. If at any time he shows his displeasure or wants to leave, don't keep him against his will. Have another try later.

2. Start by gently petting him all over whilst talking to him softly to keep him calm.

3. Moving down from the top of his head to his shoulder, massage in circular motions. Keep the pressure gentle.

4. Next, move onto his chest and front legs. If he's not keen on you touching his legs, then simply move on. Don't break the spell!

5. Massage in circular motions along his back, on both sides of the spine. Finally, slowly move onto his back legs (again, leave these if he doesn't enjoy it) and tail area.

6. In just 10 minutes, you should have a de-stressed, truly pampered dog. If only he could return the favour!

You can use massage in situations where your dog is getting stressed, for example when there's a thunderstorm brewing and even for a pre-walk warm up (in the same way humans limber up before exercise). Very much like grooming, the health benefits of massage include:

- discovering unknown lumps, bumps and injuries
- relieving joint and muscle pain and aches
- detecting ticks and other parasites
- improving circulation and blood flow to the muscles, skin and major organs
- stimulating the lymph system to help eliminate toxins
- improving the quality of the coat
- producing deep relaxation (both in you and your dog!).

Happiness is a

warm puppy.

CHARLES SCHULZ